The Millionaire Code

A systematic approach comprising 9 steps to increase your financial growth and build wealth

Andrew Taylor

Copyright © 2024 By Andrew Taylor

All rights reserved. No part of this publication may be reproduced, distributed, or transmitted in any form or by any means, including photocopying, recording, or other electronic or mechanical methods, without the prior written permission of the publisher, except in the case of brief quotations embodied in critical reviews and certain other noncommercial uses permitted by copyright law

TABLE OF CONTENTS

Table of contents 3

Introduction 5

Chapter 1 9

    Financial Zero Point 9

Chapter 2 15

    Wealth Building Mentality 15

Chapter 3 21

    The Path To Wealth Creation 21

Chapter 4 29

    Strategies For Growing Wealth 29

Chapter 5 37

    Creating Multiple Income Streams 37

Chapter 6 45

Optimizing Your Income And Expenses To Reduce Debt 45

Chapter 7 53

The Philanthropy Giving Back And Social Impact In Business 53

Chapter 8 61

Networking And Strategic Partnership For Expansion 61

Chapter 9 69

Protecting And Sustaining The Wealth 69

Conclusion 76

INTRODUCTION

Imagine waking up one morning, stretching your arms wide, and feeling that delicious weight of financial freedom settle over you. No more worries about paying bills or living paycheck to paycheck. Just you and an abundance mindset, ready to embrace all the juicy opportunities life has to offer.

Yeah, is that what you're thinking - "Sounds like a dream, buddy." But stick with me here, because I'm about to share the millionaire code that could turn that dream into your reality. It's not some get-rich-quick scheme or shady pyramid thing. Nope, this is a systematic, step-by-step approach that will help you enhance your financial growth and build serious wealth.

Now, there is no need to lie to you - this path isn't a walk in the park. It'll take hard work, discipline, and a willingness to think outside the box. But if you're ready to ditch the mediocre and embrace the millionaire mindset, then strap in, because this ride is about to get wild.

First things first, we need to talk about your "why." Why do you want to be a millionaire? Is it to travel the world without a care? To provide for your family in ways you never could before? Or maybe you just want the freedom to pursue your passions without money holding you back. Whatever your reason, it needs to be crystal clear in your mind, because that "why" will be your guiding light on this journey.

Once you've nailed down your "why," it's time to start unpacking the millionaire code itself. And let me tell you, this thing is like a finely tuned machine, with nine precise steps that work together to propel you toward financial freedom.

Step one is all about mastering your money mindset. We're not just talking about budgeting and saving here (although those are important too). No, we're diving deep into the psychology of wealth, breaking down the limiting beliefs and self-sabotaging behaviors that have been holding you back.

From there, we'll move on to step two, where you'll learn how to create multiple streams of income. Because let's be real, relying on a single paycheck is like trying to build a skyscraper on a foundation of sand. Diversifying your income sources is key to building lasting wealth.

And that's just the tip of the iceberg, my friend. Throughout the next seven steps, we'll cover everything from zero to millionaire secrets to entrepreneurial mindsets. Each step builds upon the last until you've got a rock-solid foundation for financial success.

"This all sounds great, but how do I know it works?" Fair question, my friend. But here's the thing - this code isn't just some theory cooked up in an ivory tower. It's a battle-tested system that has been proven time and time to work for people in all businesses. The point is, this stuff works. And it can work for you too, if you're willing to put in the effort and follow the steps.

So, what do you say? Are you ready to unlock the millionaire code and start building the life of your dreams? It won't be easy, but the payoff will be worth it. Just imagine waking up every morning with that delicious weight of financial freedom settled over you, free to embrace all the juicy opportunities life has to offer.

The choice is yours, my friend. But if you're ready to leap, then buckle up, because this is just the beginning of an adventure that could change your life forever.

CHAPTER 1

Financial Zero Point

The financial zero point can be thought of as the point at which an individual's income matches their expenses, resulting in a balance between inflows and outflows of money. It is a state where one's financial obligations are met without reliance on debt or external assistance.

Achieving the financial zero point signifies financial independence, where an individual no longer lives paycheck to paycheck and has the freedom to allocate resources towards long-term goals, such as savings, investments, or personal growth.

Implications of the Financial Zero Point:

1. **Reduced Financial Stress:** One of the primary benefits of reaching the financial zero point is a significant reduction in financial stress. Living in a constant state of financial insecurity can have detrimental effects on mental health and overall well-being. By achieving financial

equilibrium, individuals can experience a sense of stability and peace of mind.

2. **Increased Financial Freedom:** Attaining the financial zero point provides individuals with increased financial freedom. Freed from the burden of debt and financial obligations, they gain the flexibility to make choices based on personal preferences rather than financial constraints. This newfound freedom can lead to a higher quality of life and increased opportunities for personal and professional growth.

3. **Enhanced Long-Term Financial Security:** The financial zero point is closely tied to long-term financial security. By achieving a balance between income and expenses, individuals can allocate resources toward building an emergency fund, retirement savings, or investments. This paves the way for a more secure financial future, reducing the vulnerability to unexpected financial shocks.

Strategies for Approaching the Financial Zero Point:

1. **Budgeting and Expense Tracking:** The cornerstone of attaining the financial zero point is effective budgeting. Creating a comprehensive budget helps individuals gain a clear understanding of their income, expenses, and spending habits. By tracking expenses meticulously, one can identify areas where adjustments can be made to achieve financial equilibrium.

2. **Reducing Debt:** Managing and reducing debt is crucial when striving for the financial zero point. High-interest debt can be a significant barrier to achieving financial equilibrium. Prioritizing debt repayment, exploring debt consolidation options, and adopting prudent borrowing practices can expedite the journey toward financial independence.

3. **Increasing Income:** Another approach to reaching the financial zero point is by increasing income streams. This can be accomplished through various means, such as seeking career advancement opportunities,

acquiring new skills, starting a side business, or pursuing investment options that generate passive income. Diversifying income sources can help individuals accelerate their progress toward financial equilibrium.

4. **Embracing Minimalism and Conscious Spending:** Adopting a minimalist mindset and practicing conscious spending are essential components of the financial zero-point journey. By distinguishing between needs and wants and making deliberate choices about expenditure, individuals can optimize their resources and ensure that their expenses align with their values and long-term goals.

The financial zero point represents a paradigm shift in our understanding of personal finance. It is a state of equilibrium where income matches expenses, enabling individuals to experience reduced financial stress, increased freedom, and enhanced long-term financial security.

While achieving the financial zero point may require discipline, strategic planning, and lifestyle adjustments, the benefits it offers are invaluable. By implementing effective budgeting, reducing debt, increasing income, and embracing conscious spending, individuals can embark on a transformative journey toward financial independence.

CHAPTER 2

Wealth Building Mentality

In today's world, many individuals aspire to achieve financial freedom and build lasting wealth. While there are various strategies and approaches to wealth building, one crucial factor that sets successful individuals apart is their mindset. The wealth-building mentality encompasses a set of attitudes, beliefs, and habits that create a solid foundation for financial success.

The key principles of the wealth-building mentality and explore how adopting this mindset can positively impact your financial journey.

1. Shifting from a Scarcity Mindset to an Abundance Mindset

The first step in developing a wealth-building mentality is to shift from a scarcity mindset to an abundance mindset. A scarcity mindset is rooted in the belief that there is a limited amount of resources and opportunities available. On the other hand, an abundance mindset recognizes that opportunities, wealth, and resources are abundant in the world.

By embracing an abundance mindset, individuals open themselves up to new possibilities and are more likely to seize opportunities that come their way. They have a strong belief in their capacity to generate wealth and are willing to take calculated risks to attain their financial objectives.

2. Setting Clear Financial Goals

Having clear and well-defined financial goals is another essential aspect of the wealth-building mentality. Successful individuals have a clear vision of what they want to achieve financially, whether it's saving for retirement, starting a business, or buying a home. By setting specific, measurable, achievable, relevant, and time-bound (SMART) goals, individuals can create a roadmap to guide their financial decisions and actions.

3. Cultivating a Continuous Learning Mindset

The pursuit of knowledge and continuous learning is a hallmark of the wealth-building mentality. Successful individuals understand the importance of acquiring financial literacy and staying informed about investment strategies, market trends, and personal finance principles. They read books, attend seminars, listen to podcasts, and seek advice from mentors to expand their knowledge base.

By continuously learning and adapting to new information, individuals can make informed financial decisions and identify opportunities that others may overlook. This willingness to learn and adapt is crucial in an ever-changing economic landscape.

4. Embracing Delayed Gratification

Delayed gratification is a fundamental principle of wealth building. It involves having the discipline to forgo immediate pleasures and instead invest time, effort, and resources in activities that will yield long-term benefits. This could mean saving a portion of income, investing in appreciating assets or reinvesting profits back into a business.

By practicing delayed gratification, individuals can accumulate wealth over time and enjoy the fruits of their labor in the future. This mindset shift requires discipline, self-control, and a focus on long-term goals rather than short-term gratification.

5. Developing a Strong Work Ethic

Building wealth requires hard work and a strong work ethic. Successful individuals understand that there are no shortcuts to financial success and are willing to put in the necessary effort to achieve their goals. They are proactive, persistent, and committed to their vision, often going above and beyond what is expected of them.

A strong work ethic involves being diligent, taking initiative, and constantly seeking ways to improve one's skills and productivity. By consistently delivering value and striving for excellence in their chosen field, individuals increase their chances of financial success.

6. Building a Supportive Network

The wealth-building mentality also emphasizes the importance of surrounding oneself with like-minded individuals who support and inspire financial growth. A strong support network can offer valuable perspectives, and guidance, and help keep you accountable. By connecting with individuals who have achieved financial success or share similar goals, individuals can leverage their knowledge and experiences to accelerate their wealth-building journey.

7. Overcoming Fear of Failure

Fear of failure can be a significant barrier to wealth building. The wealth-building mentality involves embracing failure as an opportunity for growth and learning. Successful individuals understand that setbacks and challenges are inevitable, but they view them as valuable lessons rather than insurmountable obstacles.

By reframing failure as a stepping stone to success, individuals can develop resilience, perseverance, and the ability to bounce back from setbacks. This mindset shift allows them to take calculated risks, learn from their mistakes, and adapt their strategies as needed.

The wealth-building mentality encompasses a collection of attitudes, beliefs, and habits that pave the way for financial success. By adopting an abundance mindset, setting clear goals, continuously learning, embracing delayed gratification, cultivating a strong work ethic, building a supportive network, and overcoming the fear of failure, individuals can develop a mindset that propels them toward their financial aspirations.

While the wealth-building mentality is not a guarantee of instant wealth, it provides a solid foundation for long-term financial success. By incorporating these principles into your life, you can unlock your potential, make informed financial decisions, and create a path toward building lasting wealth.

CHAPTER 3

The Path To Wealth Creation

Wealth creation refers to the process of accumulating assets and resources that have long-term value. It involves growing one's financial net worth over time by generating income and increasing the value of investments. While there are various means of wealth creation, such as entrepreneurship or inheritance, investing is a fundamental tool accessible to individuals at different income levels.

The Importance of Investing

Investing is crucial for wealth creation due to several reasons. First, it offers the potential for higher returns compared to traditional saving methods like keeping money in a bank account. By investing in assets such as stocks, real estate, or bonds, individuals can benefit from the power of compounding and capital appreciation. Second, investing provides a hedge against inflation, as the returns from investments have the potential to outpace the eroding effects of rising prices over time. Lastly, investing allows individuals to diversify their income sources and build a passive income stream, which can lead to financial independence and security.

Key Principles of Investing

1. Setting Clear Financial Goals: Before embarking on an investment journey, it is crucial to define specific financial goals. This includes determining the time horizon for investments, risk tolerance, and desired outcomes. Clear goals help shape investment strategies and provide a benchmark for measuring success.

2. Building a Solid Foundation: Building a strong financial foundation is essential before diving into investments. This includes establishing an emergency fund to cover unforeseen expenses and paying off high-interest debts. By creating a solid financial base, individuals can mitigate risk and have a stable platform for wealth creation.

3. **Diversification:** Diversification is a key principle to manage risk and optimize returns. Diversification is the key strategy for allocating investments across various asset classes, industries, and geographical regions. Diversification helps reduce the impact of volatility in any one investment and increases the likelihood of capturing positive returns from various sources.

4. **Long-Term Perspective:** Investing is a long-term endeavor. Successful investors understand that wealth creation requires patience, discipline, and a focus on long-term goals. Short-term market fluctuations and noise should not deter investors from sticking to their investment plans.

Investment Strategies

1. **Stocks:** Investing in stocks offers individuals an opportunity to own a portion of a company's ownership and participate in its growth. Stock investments can be made through individual stocks or diversified portfolios such as mutual funds or exchange-traded funds (ETFs). It is important to conduct thorough research, analyze

financial statements, and consider factors such as company fundamentals, industry trends, and market conditions.

2. Bonds: Bonds are fixed-income securities issued by governments, municipalities, or corporations. Our organization offers bonds that provide regular interest payments and return the principal amount upon maturity. Bonds are widely regarded as a lower-risk investment compared to stocks, and they offer a reliable source of income. Bonds are generally considered less risky than stocks and can provide a steady income stream. However, it is crucial to assess creditworthiness, interest rate risk, and inflationary pressures when investing in bonds.

3. Real Estate: Investing in real estate can provide both income and capital appreciation. One can achieve property ownership through direct ownership, investment in real estate investment trusts (REITs), or utilizing real estate crowdfunding platforms. Real estate investments require careful evaluation of location, market trends, rental income potential, and maintenance costs.

4. **Index Funds:** Index funds are passively managed investment vehicles that aim to replicate the performance of a specific market index, such as the S&P 500. They offer broad market exposure, diversification, and lower fees compared to actively managed funds. Index funds are suitable for those seeking a long-term, low-cost investment strategy.

Potential Pitfalls and Risks

1. **Lack of Knowledge:** Insufficient knowledge and understanding of investment products and strategies can lead to poor decision-making. It is crucial to educate oneself about various investment options, market dynamics, and risk factors before committing capital.

2. **Emotional Investing:** Allowing emotions to drive investment decisions can be detrimental. Fear and greed often lead individuals to buy at market peaks and sell during downturns, resulting in poor returns. Developing a

disciplined and rational approach to investing is essential for long-term success.

3. **Overlooking Risk Management:** Failing to assess and manage risks can expose investors to significant losses. It is important to conduct thorough due diligence, diversify investments, and set appropriate stop-loss or exit strategies.

4. **Timing the Market:** Attempting to time the market by predicting short-term price movements is challenging and often counterproductive. Successful investing focuses on time in the market rather than timing the market. Engaging in consistent and disciplined long-term investing tends to generate superior outcomes.

The path to wealth creation through investing is both exciting and challenging. It requires individuals to acquire knowledge, develop the right mindset, and implement sound strategies. By understanding the key principles of investing, setting clear financial goals, and diversifying investments, individuals can increase their chances of building wealth over time.

It is important to remember that investing is a long-term journey, and success does not come overnight. Patience, discipline, and the ability to withstand market fluctuations are crucial. Additionally, investors should be aware of potential pitfalls such as lack of knowledge, emotional decision-making, and inadequate risk management.

Ultimately, the path to wealth creation through investing is unique for each individual. It requires continuous learning, adaptability, and periodic evaluation of investment strategies. By following the principles outlined in this article and staying focused on long-term goals, individuals can embark on a rewarding journey toward financial freedom and wealth creation.

CHAPTER 4

Strategies For Growing Wealth

In today's fast-paced world, achieving financial success and growing wealth has become a significant goal for many individuals. While the concept of wealth may vary from person to person, the underlying desire remains the same—to secure a comfortable and prosperous future. Fortunately, numerous strategies can help individuals navigate the path to financial success.

The key strategies for growing wealth and providing actionable insights to assist you in your journey toward financial prosperity.

1. Develop a Financial Plan

A well-defined financial plan serves as the foundation for growing wealth. It involves setting clear financial goals, creating a budget, and establishing a roadmap to achieve those goals. Start by assessing your current financial situation, including your income, expenses, debts, and assets. Once you have a clear understanding of your financial standing, set realistic short-term and long-term goals. Whether it's saving for retirement, purchasing a home, or starting a business, your goals will shape your wealth-building strategy.

2. Save and Invest Wisely

Developing a habit of saving money is an essential foundation for accumulating wealth over time. Start by creating an emergency fund to cover unforeseen expenses, such as medical bills or job loss. Aim to save at least three to six months' worth of living expenses in this fund. Additionally, develop a habit of consistent saving by automating your savings and allocating a portion of your income towards your savings goals.

However, saving alone may not be sufficient to grow wealth significantly. Investing wisely is equally crucial. To effectively manage risk, it is advisable to diversify your investments across various asset classes, including stocks, bonds, and real estate. Educate yourself about investment options, seek advice from financial professionals, and stay informed about market trends. Remember, investing is a long-term strategy, and it's essential to be patient and avoid impulsive decisions.

3. Minimize Debt and Manage Credit

To accelerate wealth growth, it is essential to minimize debt and manage credit responsibly. High-interest debts, such as credit card debt, can hinder your financial progress. To effectively manage your debts, it is recommended to prioritize paying off the debts with the highest interest rates first. Meanwhile, you can continue making minimum payments on your other debts. This strategy helps minimize the overall interest costs and accelerate your progress toward debt freedom. Consider debt consolidation strategies or balance transfers to reduce interest payments.

Simultaneously, managing credit responsibly is crucial for long-term financial success. Pay your bills on time, maintain a good credit score, and avoid unnecessary debt. A strong credit history will enable you to access better interest rates and financial opportunities in the future.

4. Increase Earnings and Seek Additional Income Streams

Growing wealth isn't solely about cutting expenses; it also involves increasing your earning potential. Invest in yourself by acquiring new skills, pursuing additional education, or taking up side hustles. Leverage your strengths and explore opportunities for career advancement or entrepreneurship. Diversifying your income streams can provide stability and accelerate your wealth-building journey.

5. Leverage Tax-Advantaged Accounts

Understanding tax laws and utilizing tax-advantaged accounts can significantly impact your wealth growth. Take advantage of retirement accounts like 401(k)s or IRAs, which offer tax benefits and potential employer matches. Maximize contributions to these accounts to benefit from tax deferrals and compound growth over time.

Additionally, explore other tax-efficient investment options such as Health Savings Accounts (HSAs) or 529 college savings plans. These accounts offer tax advantages and can help you save for medical expenses or education costs while reducing your tax liability.

6. Continuously Educate Yourself

Financial knowledge is a powerful tool for wealth building. Stay informed about personal finance topics, investment strategies, and emerging trends. Read books, attend seminars or webinars, and follow reputable financial experts to expand your understanding of wealth management. With a solid foundation of knowledge, you can make informed decisions and adapt your strategies as the financial landscape evolves.

7. Protect Your Wealth

Safeguarding your wealth is as important as growing it. Mitigate risks by obtaining adequate insurance coverage for your health, life, home, and other valuable assets. Regularly review your insurance policies to ensure they align with your current needs and circumstances. Estate planning is also essential to protect your wealth for future generations. Consult with professionals to create a comprehensive estate plan that includes wills, trusts, and power of attorney documents.

8. Practice Discipline and Patience

Growing wealth is a long-term endeavor that requires discipline and patience. Avoid get-rich-quick schemes or impulsive investments promising unrealistic returns. Stick to your financial plan, maintain a disciplined saving and investment strategy, and be patient while allowing compound interest and market forces to work in your favor.

Growing wealth is an achievable goal with the right strategies and mindset. By developing a financial plan, saving and investing wisely, minimizing debt, increasing earnings, leveraging tax-advantaged accounts, continuously educating yourself, protecting your wealth, and practicing discipline, you can unlock the path to financial success. Remember, everyone's journey is unique, and it's essential to adapt these strategies to your specific circumstances. With perseverance and a long-term perspective, you can embark on a fulfilling and prosperous wealth-building journey.

CHAPTER 5

Creating Multiple Income Streams

In the current dynamic economic environment, depending solely on one income stream can pose a significant risk. Economic downturns, job insecurity, and unexpected expenses can quickly disrupt financial stability. To mitigate these risks, individuals are increasingly turning to the concept of creating multiple income streams through diversification. Diversifying income involves generating revenue from various sources, which not only bolsters financial security but also opens up opportunities for growth and wealth creation.

The importance of creating multiple income streams and providing actionable insights on how to effectively diversify your income.

1. **Understanding the Importance of Diversification:**

Diversification is a fundamental principle in finance, and it holds when it comes to income as well. By diversifying income streams, individuals can reduce their vulnerability to financial shocks and enhance their overall financial well-being. Relying solely on a single job or income source exposes individuals to the risk of unemployment, industry-specific downturns, or technological disruptions. Creating multiple income streams acts as a safety net, ensuring that even if one source falters, others can continue providing financial support.

2. **Types of Income Streams:**

   - **Earned Income:** This type of income is earned through active participation in a job or business. It includes salaries, wages, and self-employment income. While earned income is the most common source, it is essential to explore other types to diversify effectively.

- **Passive Income:** Passive income is generated from assets or investments that require minimal effort to maintain or manage. Examples include rental properties, dividends from investments, or royalties from creative works. Passive income provides ongoing cash flow and can be a significant component of a diversified income portfolio.

- **Portfolio Income:** Portfolio income is derived from investments such as stocks, bonds, mutual funds, or real estate. It includes capital gains, interest, and dividends. Building a diversified investment portfolio can contribute to long-term wealth accumulation and provide income streams independent of traditional employment.

- **Side Hustles:** Side hustles refer to part-time or flexible ventures pursued alongside a primary job. They can range from freelancing, consulting, online businesses, or monetizing hobbies and skills. Side hustles allow individuals to explore their passions, generate additional income, and potentially transition into full-time entrepreneurial endeavors.

3. **Benefits of Creating Multiple Income Streams:**

   - **Financial Security:** Diversifying income reduces reliance on a single source, minimizing the impact of job loss or economic downturns. Even if one income stream falters, others can provide stability and cover expenses.

   - **Increased Income Potential:** Creating multiple income streams can boost overall earning potential. By leveraging various sources, individuals can tap into new revenue streams and capitalize on different market opportunities.

- **Flexibility and Freedom:** Diversified income provides flexibility, allowing individuals to explore new interests, take risks, or pursue passion projects without the fear of financial instability. It offers individuals the opportunity to prioritize personal fulfillment over financial obligations, empowering them to make choices based on their desires.

- **Skill Development:** Pursuing diverse income streams often requires developing new skills and knowledge. This continuous learning process enhances personal and professional growth, making individuals more adaptable and resilient in an ever-evolving job market.

4. **Strategies for Diversifying Income:**

- **Identify Your Strengths:** Start by evaluating your skills, interests, and assets. Determine what unique abilities or resources you possess that can be monetized. This self-assessment will help identify potential income streams that align with your strengths.

- **Explore New Opportunities:** Research market trends, emerging industries, and areas of growth. Look for opportunities to leverage your skills or invest in assets that can generate passive or portfolio income. Stay open to new ideas and be willing to step outside your comfort zone.

- **Build a Side Hustle:** Consider starting a part-time business or freelancing in your area of expertise. This can be an excellent way to test the viability of a new venture while maintaining the security of your primary income source.

- **Invest Wisely**: Learn about investment options and seek professional advice if needed. Diversify your investment portfolio by allocating funds to different asset classes, such as stocks, bonds, real estate, or mutual funds. Regularly review and rebalance your investments to ensure optimal returns.

- **Leverage the Power of the Internet:** The Internet has opened up a plethora of opportunities for generating income. Explore online platforms, such as e-commerce, affiliate marketing, content creation, or online tutoring, to tap into a global market and diversify your income streams.

- **Continual Learning and Adaptation:** Embrace a growth mindset and commit to lifelong learning. Acquire new skills, stay updated with industry trends, and adapt to changing market demands. This proactive approach will ensure your income streams remain relevant and resilient.

Creating multiple income streams through diversification is a proactive approach to financial stability, growth, and freedom. By embracing various income sources such as earned income, passive income, portfolio income, and side hustles, individuals can protect themselves from financial risks, increase their earning potential, and explore new opportunities. Diversification requires careful planning, self-assessment, and a willingness to step outside one's comfort zone.

By implementing the strategies outlined in this article, individuals can create a robust and resilient income portfolio that not only provides financial security but also opens doors to personal and professional growth. Remember, diversification is not a one-time task but an ongoing process that requires adaptability, continuous learning, and a proactive mindset. Start today and unlock the power of multiple income streams for a brighter financial future.

CHAPTER 6

Optimizing Your Income And Expenses To Reduce Debt

Managing personal finances is an essential skill that can significantly impact our lives. One crucial aspect of financial management is optimizing your income and expenses to reduce debt. This practice involves strategically managing your earnings and expenditures to ensure a healthy financial future.

The effective strategies for increasing income and reducing expenses to minimize debt and achieve financial stability.

1. Assessing Your Financial Situation

Before embarking on any debt reduction plan, it is vital to assess your current financial situation. Start by evaluating your income sources, including your salary, investments, and any additional sources of revenue. Simultaneously, analyze your expenses by categorizing them into fixed (e.g., rent, utilities) and variable (e.g., groceries, entertainment) costs. This assessment will provide a clear picture of your financial health and act as a foundation for optimizing your income and expenses.

2. **Increasing Your Income**

   - **Enhance Your Skills:** To increase your earning potential, consider investing in acquiring new skills or enhancing existing ones. This could involve taking relevant courses, attending workshops, or pursuing advanced degrees. By improving your skills, you can become more competitive in the job market, opening doors to higher-paying positions.

   - **Seek a Promotion or a New Job:** Assess your current job and explore opportunities for growth within your organization. Consider discussing your career aspirations with your supervisor and express your interest in taking on additional responsibilities. Alternatively, if growth prospects are limited, explore job openings in your field that offer better compensation packages.

- **Explore Side Hustles:** Supplementing your primary income with a side hustle can significantly boost your overall earnings. Identify your skills and hobbies that can be monetized and explore opportunities such as freelancing, consulting, or starting a small business. The gig economy offers a plethora of options to earn extra income and accelerate debt reduction.

- **Passive Income Sources:** Investigate avenues for generating passive income, such as investing in stocks, bonds, or real estate. Passive income streams can provide a consistent flow of money without requiring substantial time and effort, ultimately helping to alleviate debt burdens.

3. **Reducing Expenses**

   ➢ **Create a Budget:** Developing a comprehensive budget is crucial for monitoring and controlling your expenses. Track your spending patterns for a few months and identify areas where you can cut back. Categorize your expenses into fixed and variable costs, and allocate a specific amount for each category. Stick to your budget to ensure a disciplined approach to expenditure.

   ➢ **Minimize Discretionary Spending:** Evaluate your discretionary expenses, such as dining out, entertainment, and shopping. Consider reducing these expenses by finding cost-effective alternatives or temporarily eliminating unnecessary purchases. Making minor adjustments to our daily habits can result in substantial long-term savings.

- **Negotiate Bills and Contracts:** Review your recurring bills, such as utilities, cable, and internet services. Contact your providers and negotiate better rates or explore alternative service providers that offer competitive pricing. Similarly, reassess your insurance policies, cell phone plans, and subscription services to identify potential cost-saving opportunities.

- **Cut Down on Debt-Inducing Habits:** Identify habits that contribute to debt accumulation, such as excessive credit card usage or impulse buying. Make a conscious effort to curb these behaviors by adopting a cash-only approach or using debit cards instead of credit cards. This practice will assist you in maintaining financial stability and prevent the accumulation of unnecessary debt.

4. Debt Repayment Strategies

- **Snowball Method:** The snowball method involves paying off debts starting with the smallest balance while making minimum payments on other debts. Once you have paid off the smallest debt, allocate the amount you were paying towards the next smallest debt. This strategy offers a psychological advantage as you progressively eliminate debts, which serves as a motivator to persist in your debt-reduction endeavors.

- **Avalanche Method:** The avalanche method prioritizes the repayment of debts with the highest interest rates. By targeting high-interest debts, you minimize the amount of interest accrued over time and accelerate the overall debt repayment process. Make minimum payments on all debts while allocating extra funds towards the debt with the highest interest rate.

- **Debt Consolidation:** Consider consolidating multiple debts into a single loan with a lower interest rate. Debt consolidation simplifies repayment by combining various debts into one monthly payment. However, it is essential to carefully evaluate the terms and conditions of the consolidation loan to ensure it is financially advantageous.

Optimizing your income and expenses to reduce debt requires a holistic approach to personal finance management. By assessing your financial situation, increasing your income, reducing expenses, and implementing effective debt repayment strategies, you can regain control of your finances and achieve long-term financial stability. Remember, the journey toward debt reduction requires discipline, perseverance, and a commitment to making informed financial decisions.

CHAPTER 7

The Philanthropy Giving Back And Social Impact In Business

Philanthropy, giving back, and social impact are integral components of a thriving society. In recent years, businesses worldwide have recognized the significance of these practices, not only as acts of goodwill but also as strategies to foster positive change and enhance their overall reputation.

The concept of philanthropy, its role in business, and the transformative social impact it can have.

I. Understanding Philanthropy:

Philanthropy can be defined as the act of promoting the welfare of others, typically through charitable donations or actions. It stems from a deep sense of compassion and a desire to make a positive difference in the lives of others. While philanthropy is often associated with wealthy individuals or foundations, businesses have also embraced this practice, leveraging their resources to address societal issues and contribute to the greater good.

II. The Role of Philanthropy in Business:

1. Corporate Social Responsibility (CSR):

Philanthropy forms a crucial aspect of corporate social responsibility (CSR), which is the commitment of businesses to operate ethically and contribute to sustainable development. By engaging in philanthropic initiatives, companies demonstrate their dedication to the well-being of society beyond their financial bottom line.

2. Reputation and Brand Enhancement:

Engaging in philanthropy can greatly improve a company's reputation and brand image. Socially responsible actions resonate with consumers, who increasingly prioritize ethical businesses. By giving back, companies build trust, loyalty, and positive associations with their brand, ultimately leading to increased customer engagement and market competitiveness.

3. Employee Engagement and Retention:

Philanthropic initiatives also impact employees. By aligning with a company's philanthropic values, employees feel a sense of purpose and pride in their work. This, in turn, fosters higher levels of engagement and improves employee retention rates. Additionally, employee volunteer programs and corporate giving campaigns can promote teamwork, boost morale, and create a positive work environment.

III. Types of Philanthropic Initiatives:

1. Corporate Donations:

One of the most common forms of philanthropy in business is monetary donations. Businesses often allocate a portion of their profits toward supporting charitable causes. These donations can be directed to a wide range of organizations, including nonprofits, community development programs, educational institutions, environmental initiatives, and healthcare initiatives.

2. In-Kind Donations:

In addition to financial contributions, businesses often provide in-kind donations, such as products, services, or expertise. This form of philanthropy allows companies to leverage their core competencies to address specific societal needs. For example, a technology firm can donate equipment to schools, or a healthcare company can offer free medical services in underserved areas.

3. Employee Volunteerism:

Encouraging employee volunteerism is another powerful way for businesses to give back. Companies can organize volunteer programs that enable employees to contribute their time and skills to charitable projects. This not only benefits the communities being served but also empowers employees, fostering personal growth, and a sense of fulfillment.

IV. Measuring Social Impact:

To ensure the effectiveness of philanthropic efforts, businesses need to measure their social impact. This involves setting clear goals, defining key performance indicators (KPIs), and monitoring progress. By evaluating outcomes, companies can refine their strategies, maximize their positive influence, and make data-driven decisions regarding future philanthropic endeavors.

V. Challenges and Future Trends:

1. Scalability and Sustainability:

One challenge business face in philanthropy is achieving scalability and sustainability. While individual acts of giving can make a difference, long-term impact requires strategic planning, partnerships, and a focus on systemic change. Businesses need to explore innovative models that go beyond one-time donations to create lasting solutions.

2. Collaboration and Collective Impact:

To address complex social issues effectively, collaboration is crucial. Businesses can join forces with other organizations, nonprofits, government entities, and community stakeholders to maximize their impact. This collective approach, known as collective impact, harnesses the diverse strengths and resources of multiple entities to drive meaningful change.

3. Socially Responsible Investing:

An emerging trend in philanthropy is socially responsible investing (SRI). SRI involves investing in companies that align with specific social or environmental goals, promoting positive change through financial support. This approach allows businesses to integrate their philanthropic values into their investment strategies, creating a more sustainable and ethical financial ecosystem.

Philanthropy, giving back, and social impact have become integral aspects of modern business practices. By embracing philanthropy, companies can enhance their reputation, engage and retain employees, and contribute to the betterment of society.

Through various initiatives, businesses can make a lasting social impact, addressing critical issues and forging a brighter future for all. As the landscape of philanthropy continues to evolve, collaboration, measurement of social impact, and sustainable practices will shape the future of giving back in business.

CHAPTER 8

Networking And Strategic Partnership For Expansion

In today's interconnected and competitive business landscape, networking and strategic partnerships have emerged as vital tools for organizations seeking to expand their operations and unlock new growth opportunities the significance of networking and strategic partnerships, highlighting their benefits, key considerations, and effective strategies to foster successful collaborations.

By understanding the power of networking and strategic partnerships, businesses can leverage collective strengths, access new markets, and drive sustainable growth.

I. The Importance of Networking:

Networking forms the foundation for establishing valuable connections and building relationships within the business ecosystem. It involves actively engaging with individuals, industry experts, and potential partners to exchange ideas, information, and resources.

The benefits of networking include:

- **Knowledge Exchange:** Networking provides opportunities to learn from industry peers, stay updated with trends, and gain insights into best practices. By connecting with experts and thought leaders, organizations can acquire valuable knowledge that can drive innovation and competitiveness.

- **Business Opportunities:** Networking opens doors to new business opportunities, including partnerships, collaborations, and joint ventures. It enables companies to tap into a wider network of potential customers, suppliers, investors, and distributors, expanding their reach and market presence.

- **Access to Resources:** Through networking, organizations can access a diverse pool of resources, such as talent, funding, technology, and infrastructure. Collaboration with complementary businesses allows for shared resources, reducing costs and enhancing operational efficiency.

II. Strategic Partnerships for Expansion:

Strategic partnerships involve formal collaborations between two or more organizations, driven by shared goals, mutual benefits, and complementary capabilities. When executed effectively, strategic partnerships can fuel growth and facilitate market expansion.

Here's why strategic partnerships are crucial:

- **Market Access and Expansion:** Strategic partnerships enable businesses to enter new markets or expand their existing market presence. By leveraging the partner's established customer base, distribution channels, or market knowledge, organizations can overcome entry barriers and reach a broader audience effectively.

➢ **Resource and Capability Sharing:** Partnerships allow organizations to pool resources, expertise, and capabilities, unlocking synergistic benefits. For example, a technology company partnering with a manufacturing firm can combine their strengths to develop innovative products and access new markets.

➢ **Risk Mitigation:** Strategic partnerships can help mitigate risks associated with new ventures. By sharing costs, responsibilities, and market intelligence, organizations can navigate uncertainties and reduce the burden of individual investments.

III. Key Considerations for Networking and Strategic Partnerships:

While networking and strategic partnerships offer immense potential, they require careful planning and consideration. Here are some key factors to keep in mind:

- **Alignment of Goals and Values:** Successful partnerships are built on a shared vision, aligned goals, and compatible values. It is crucial to assess the partner's strategic fit, ensuring their objectives and values align with your organization's mission.

- **Complementary Capabilities:** Partnerships should bring together organizations with complementary capabilities and resources. This synergy allows for the creation of unique value propositions, fostering innovation and competitive advantage.

- **Clear Communication and Trust:** Open and transparent communication is essential for building trust and maintaining a healthy partnership. Establishing clear expectations, roles, and responsibilities from the outset reduces the likelihood of misunderstandings and conflicts.

- **Mutually Beneficial Agreements:** The partnership agreement should outline mutually beneficial terms, including resource sharing, revenue sharing, intellectual property rights, and dispute resolution mechanisms. A clearly defined agreement safeguards the interests of all parties involved.

IV. Strategies for Successful Networking and Strategic Partnerships:

To maximize the potential of networking and strategic partnerships, organizations can implement the following strategies:

➢ **Active Participation in Industry Events:** Attending conferences, trade shows, and industry events provides opportunities to meet like-minded professionals, explore potential collaborations, and stay informed about industry trends.

➢ **Online Networking:** Leveraging digital platforms, such as LinkedIn, industry forums, and social media groups, expands the reach of networking efforts. Engaging in online discussions, sharing insights, and building relationships can lead to valuable connections.

> **Research and Due Diligence:** Conduct thorough research before entering into a partnership. Evaluate the partner's track record, reputation, financial stability, and compatibility with your organization's culture and values.

> **Continuous Relationship Building:** Networking is an ongoing process that requires consistent effort. Regularly nurture relationships with key contacts, maintain open lines of communication, and explore avenues for collaboration.

Networking and strategic partnerships are essential strategies for organizations aiming to expand their operations and unlock growth opportunities. By actively participating in networking activities, businesses can forge valuable connections, access knowledge, and identify potential partners. Strategic partnerships, on the other hand, enable organizations to leverage shared resources, expand market reach, and mitigate risks. By considering key factors and implementing effective strategies, businesses can establish successful collaborations that drive sustainable growth in today's interconnected business landscape.

CHAPTER 9

Protecting And Sustaining The Wealth

Protecting one's wealth is a crucial aspect of financial planning. Whether you have amassed substantial assets or are just starting to build y Safeguarding one's wealth is an essential element of effective financial planning. our wealth, implementing effective strategies to safeguard your financial future is essential.

The practical advice on how to protect your wealth and ensure long-term financial security.

1. Diversify Your Investments:

Diversifying your investments is a crucial principle for safeguarding wealth. It involves spreading your investments across various asset classes like stocks, bonds, real estate, and commodities. This strategy helps minimize risks by lessening the impact of any one investment's underperformance on your overall portfolio. Different asset classes perform differently under various market conditions, so diversification allows you to benefit from potential gains while minimizing potential losses.

2. Create an Emergency Fund:

Building an emergency fund is a cornerstone of financial protection. An emergency fund acts as a safety net, providing you with financial stability during unexpected events such as job loss, medical emergencies, or major repairs. It is recommended to establish an emergency fund that covers three to six months' worth of living expenses. This fund should be kept in a readily accessible account that allows for quick and easy withdrawal of funds. This fund will help you avoid dipping into your long-term investments during times of crisis.

3. Insurance Coverage:

Insurance is a crucial tool for wealth protection. Evaluate your insurance needs and ensure adequate coverage for various aspects of your life, such as health, life, disability, property, and liability. Insurance policies protect you from unforeseen expenses that could significantly impact your wealth. Regularly review your coverage to ensure it aligns with your changing circumstances and update it accordingly.

4.   Estate Planning:

Estate planning is not just for the wealthy; it is essential for anyone who wishes to protect their wealth and ensure its smooth transfer to future generations. Consult with an estate planning attorney to draft a comprehensive plan that includes a will, trusts, and powers of attorney. Proper estate planning minimizes taxes, avoids probate, and helps preserve your assets for your beneficiaries.

5.   Tax Planning:

Tax planning is a critical aspect of wealth protection. Educate yourself on the tax laws and regulations applicable to your jurisdiction. Look for legal ways to minimize your tax liabilities, such as maximizing contributions to retirement accounts, taking advantage of tax deductions and credits, and exploring tax-efficient investment strategies. Consulting with a qualified tax professional can help you navigate the complexities of tax planning.

6. **Continual Education and Financial Literacy:**

Staying informed and continually improving your financial literacy is vital for protecting your wealth. Keep abreast of economic trends, investment strategies, and regulatory changes that may affect your financial well-being. Expand your knowledge through books, reputable financial websites, seminars, and workshops. Being well-informed allows you to make sound financial decisions and adapt to changing circumstances effectively.

7. **Protect Against Identity Theft:**

In the digital age, protecting your personal and financial information is crucial. Safeguard your sensitive data by using strong, unique passwords for your online accounts, enabling two-factor authentication, and being cautious of phishing attempts. Regularly monitor your credit reports and bank statements to detect any suspicious activity. Consider using identity theft protection services to add an extra layer of security.

8. Build Strong Professional Relationships:

Building strong relationships with professionals such as financial advisors, attorneys, and accountants can provide valuable guidance in protecting your wealth. Choose qualified professionals with expertise in their respective fields who can help you make informed decisions and navigate complex financial situations. Regularly review and communicate your financial goals and concerns with your trusted advisors.

9. Maintain Adequate Liquidity:

Having sufficient liquidity ensures you can meet your financial obligations and capitalize on investment opportunities. To maintain financial stability, it is advisable to avoid accumulating excessive debt. Maintain an emergency fund, as mentioned earlier, and have a portion of your wealth readily accessible in liquid assets such as cash or highly liquid investments. This liquidity provides financial flexibility during unexpected events.

10.   Regular Portfolio Reviews:

It is important to regularly assess your investment portfolio to make sure it aligns with your financial goals and risk tolerance. If needed, adjust your portfolio to maintain the desired allocation of assets. Market conditions and personal circumstances change over time, so it's essential to adjust your investment strategy accordingly. Consider seeking professional advice to optimize your investment portfolio based on your long-term goals.

Protecting your wealth requires a proactive and holistic approach to financial planning. By diversifying your investments, creating an emergency fund, obtaining the right insurance coverage, and engaging in estate planning and tax planning, you can safeguard your assets. Additionally, continually educating yourself, protecting against identity theft, building professional relationships, maintaining liquidity, and regularly reviewing your portfolio will contribute to long-term financial security. Implementing these strategies will help you protect your wealth and ensure a prosperous future.

CONCLUSION

The Millionaire Code: A systematic approach comprising 9 steps to enhance financial growth and build wealth" provides a clear roadmap for individuals to achieve millionaire status. It emphasizes that becoming a millionaire is not a matter of luck or exclusivity, but a journey open to anyone with the right mindset, knowledge, and discipline.

The book explores a comprehensive framework of nine crucial steps designed to guide individuals toward financial abundance. From cultivating a millionaire mindset to establishing a strong financial foundation, and from harnessing passive income to leveraging investments, each step is meticulously crafted to pave the way for wealth.

A key takeaway from "The Millionaire Code" is the importance of adopting a long-term perspective. Building wealth requires patience, persistence, and wise decision-making aligned with financial goals. By implementing the principles outlined in the book, individuals can lay the groundwork for sustainable financial growth and ultimately achieve their millionaire dreams.

Continuous learning and self-improvement are also highlighted as essential aspects of wealth creation. Staying informed about the latest trends and strategies in finance is crucial to adapt to changing circumstances and take advantage of new opportunities for wealth accumulation.

The Millionaire Code underscores the power of mindset in shaping financial destiny. Believing in one's ability to succeed and maintaining a positive attitude toward money can catalyze transformative change. By adopting an abundance mindset and shedding limiting beliefs, individuals can unlock their full potential and attract wealth into their lives.

It is important to acknowledge that the journey to millionaire status comes with challenges, setbacks, and failures. However, these experiences provide valuable lessons, foster resilience, and ultimately strengthen individuals. "The Millionaire Code" encourages readers to embrace failure as an opportunity for growth and to persevere in the face of adversity.

The Millionaire Code is a comprehensive guide that equips individuals with the knowledge and tools to embark on a transformative journey toward financial abundance. By following the nine steps outlined in the book, readers can cultivate a millionaire mindset, establish a solid financial foundation, leverage passive income and investments, and navigate the complexities of wealth creation.

Building wealth is not an end in itself but a means to live a life of freedom, fulfillment, and purpose. Embrace the principles shared in this book, adapt them to your unique circumstances, and stay committed to your financial goals.

Let "The Millionaire Code" be your roadmap to financial empowerment, unlocking your potential, building wealth, and creating a lasting legacy. You possess the inherent ability to achieve financial wealth and become a millionaire. It's time to embrace it and embark on a transformative journey towards a life of abundance.

www.ingramcontent.com/pod-product-compliance
Lightning Source LLC
Chambersburg PA
CBHW050236230526
45470CB00005B/1981